D0763121

STRATEGY FOR SUCCESS
AN OUTLINE FOR PERSONAL GROWTH
S. G. McKeever

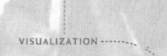

SELF-REFLECTION

GOAL-SETTING

PLANNING

FOCUS

MEDITATION

PERSEVERANCE

VISUALIZATION

HUMOR

WELL-BEING

ATTITUDE

GROWTH

TRANSFORMATION

SUCCESS

Strategy for Success

AN OUTLINE FOR PERSONAL GROWTH

S. G. McKeever

Strategy
for
Success

Editors:	Mairi McKeever
	Frank Eldredge
	Terry Eldredge
	Dhrirata Ferency
Interior Design:	Jonathan Parker
Front Cover Design:	Marina Woods
Back Cover Design:	L. R. Jennings
Back Cover Photo:	Astika Mason

ISBN 1-885-479-00-X

Third printing, 1995

For additional information contact:
McKeever Publishing
PO Box 161167
San Diego, California 92176

McKeever Publishing
San Diego • San Francisco • San Anselmo

Contents

1

East Meets West

This book was created to provide you, the reader, with a clear and concise plan for choosing and attaining your goals. To accomplish this, we will combine traditional Western theories, ideas, and plans regarding the pursuit and attainment of our material goals and desires and the views and advice given on these matters by Eastern philosophers and spiritual teachers.

By "Western" I am referring to the use of the analytical and scientific methods and their application towards technological progress and innovation. This system has dominated Western culture since the industrial revolution and has created never-before-seen technological progress.

When referring to "Eastern" philosophies I am speaking of the spiritual philosophy and world view expounded by the great spiritual teachers and philosophers of the East. This book will draw from the teachings and writings of the Buddha, the Christ, Sri Aurobindo, Swami Vivekananda, Mahatma Gandhi, Radhakrishnan, Sri Chinmoy, and Rabindranath Tagore.

Modern Western culture predominantly focuses on the attainment of material gains and desire. The industrialized Western nations have been quite successful in this respect. Eastern cultures, especially India, have traditionally given more importance to inner, or spiritual, goals. Unfortunately, the methodology of the East has often been too vague and undefined for Western minds. To unite the philosophy of the East with the methodology of the West is the purpose of this writing.

This book is about success and motivation; getting what you want out of life. It is also about the untapped awareness and potential each of us can have access to. This awareness can radically change our perception of ourselves and life, and thereby affect our feelings regarding our life and goals.

One of the classics of American success and motivational philosophy is Napoleon Hill's *Think and Grow Rich*, written in 1937 after 20 years of research involving interviews with 504 of the most successful individuals of the Western world including businessmen, inventors, and presidents. This timeless work clearly defines the ingredients necessary for the attainment of one's desires. It offers the reader a plan and strategy for making a certain amount of money or securing a fulfilling, rewarding job. It also offers ways to cultivate positive self imagery and goal setting.

In essence, it offers the reader the skills and tools necessary to attain, quickly and effectively, one's desires for money and success. The book stresses a concept that was quite revolutionary in America in 1937: the importance of positive mental attitude and visualization in the attainment of one's desires. A focused and concentrated mind was recognized by Mr. Hill as being the single most important factor in successful people. He looked at situations that most people would have called "luck" or "chance" and saw that it was actually a mental attitude that created the outcome. He was one of the first Western analysts to recognize the incredible power of a focused, concentrated, and positive mind-set.

These same principles, in various forms and disguises, are expounded upon by self-help and motivational speakers and authors to this day. Unfortunately, something is missing from this philosophy of success. Significant questions regarding the choice of goals and the effects and ramifications of various pursuits are not addressed. Also, mankind's potentialities are often severely underestimated. We often limit our awareness to material desires and neglect our spiritual possibilities.

The materialistic motivation which inspires much of our activity is never questioned. The words of Jesus offer a note of caution:

> *Therefore do not worry or say, what will we eat, or what will we drink, or with what will we be clothed?*
>
> *For worldly people seek after all these things. Your Father in heaven knows that all of these things are also necessary for you.*
>
> *But seek first the kingdom of God and his righteousness, and all those things shall be added to you.*
>
> *Therefore, do not worry about tomorrow; for tomorrow will look after itself. Sufficient for each day is its own trouble.*[1]

These Western theories regarding motivation and self-help always reference a deeper intelligence that provides a key ingredient in the attainment of one's desires. That intelligence is often called the subconscious, infinite love, intelligence, the creative force, or God. This aspect of the formuli for success is often left unexplored. Eastern philosophy deals with this subject wonderfully and can provide us with a wealth of understanding regarding this mysterious aspect of life.

Choose a desire, fixate upon it and it will be yours. This is the attitude of many motivators. We are offered the secrets of success, but little account is taken of the interconnectedness of all life and the significance of each of our desires and actions.

My uneasiness with these philosophies and practices is that they do not adequately question the unbridled pursuit of desire or the deeper significances of the pursuit. Look at America today and you can see the tragedy that results from the relentless pursuit of materialistic desire. At the same time, the West demonstrates a power and dynamism unknown to Eastern cultures, a power and dynamism that could be a great help to those nations.

Our scientific, rational understanding of the world has allowed us to create incredible technology and domination over nature. This has proven to be both a blessing and a curse. This analytical attitude toward life has also aided us in understanding the human body, although we have also lost much of our intuitive or holistic knowledge of health and healing. The scientific method has done little though when it comes to man understanding his place in this vast, mysterious world. We can analyze the distance of our solar system or the speed of light, but this knowledge has not brought us the peace of mind and heart possessed by many of the great spiritual teachers throughout history.

Eastern mystical and spiritual philosophy takes a sharply contrasting view from the Western scientific approach. Eastern philosophers and Western mystics, such as St. Thomas Aquinas and St. Augustine, say that the only desires that can bring us true, abiding happiness — which is admittedly what we all truly seek — are either the desire for God, the infinite and eternal, or the desire for the cessation of all desires. This philosophy is based on the idea that desire arises from the sense of self, from our ego. We seek to satiate our sense of self and ego through our multifarious activities. This sense of self is based on separation and distinction. "Me" as separate from all else. Therefore, seeking satisfaction for "me" serves to strengthen a sense of isolation and separation. This sense of self becomes ever stronger and separates us from the rest of the world. We soon find ourselves living estranged from other people and the world around us. The resulting sense of isolation and loneliness causes inner pain and suffering for many people. Each time we do things for other people we counteract this activity. A feeling of completeness, or oneness with life, is lost soon after childhood as we seek happiness in primarily selfish and self-centered ways. The Buddha's 2500 year-old statement, "Desire is the root of all suffering," sums up these ideas.

Admittedly, India suffers from a lack of material progress as a result of disinterest in the world bounded by time, mass, and velocity. These two contrasting philosophies of East and West leave us at extremes intellectually, emotionally, and spiritually. A uniting, middle ground needs to be explored if mankind is to find the essential, delicate balance between the spiritual realm and the physical realm necessary for healthy living. Contemporary spiritual teacher Sri Chinmoy writes:

Neither Spirit nor Matter is superior to the other. We will be far from Truth if we belittle Matter only to speak highly of Spirit. From Matter alone did our earthly cloak see the light of day.[2]

Sri Chinmoy is most likely the least known of the philosophers and teachers I will quote in this work. He was born in India in 1931. He spent twenty years, from the age of 12–32, in a spiritual community in Southern India. In 1964 he came to the United States and has since made his home in New York City. He lives in a modest home, yet has traveled throughout the world teaching peace, oneness, meditation, and the importance of service to humanity. All of this he does at no charge.

He supports himself through the worldwide sale of his books and tapes. He refers to himself as a "Student of Peace" and does not connect himself with any official group or association. This is a good indication of the depth and quality of Sri Chinmoy's philosophy and life for, as the great American philosopher Thoreau, in his masterpiece *Walden*, stated regarding the man of wealth: "[he] is always sold to the institution which makes him rich."

Sri Chinmoy's writings call for the need of both material and spiritual progress. "One without the other," he writes, "is like a bird with only one wing."

By uniting the philosophies of East and West, we will be able to draw on the best of both of these philosophies and create for ourselves an understanding that will enable us to succeed and proceed through life in a powerful yet conscious manner. The wisdom of the East and the knowledge of the West will unite in ideas and methods we can embrace to achieve our goals.

Swami Vivekananda, an Indian spiritual teacher who spoke to enthralled crowds at the Parliament of Religion in Chicago in 1893 said,

We want Europe's bright sun of intellectuality, joined with the heart of Buddha — the

wonderful, infinite heart of love and mercy. This union will give us the highest philosophy. Science and religion will meet and shake hands. Poetry and philosophy will become friends. This will be the religion of the future, and if we work it out we can be sure that it will be for all times and all peoples.[3]

Far too many people live unfulfilled lives. This needs not be the norm. We all possess the wisdom to choose fulfilling desires and the ability to attain these desires. The attainment of our desires takes effort and perseverance. There is no "miracle formula" for instant success.

By incorporating Eastern philosophy into our plans and ideas regarding success we broaden our understanding. The great American philosopher Thoreau was well versed in the ancient philosophies of the East and references these in his famous book, *Walden.*

Eastern philosophy, particularly the teachings of Sri Ramakrishna and Swami Vivekananda, has also had a profound effect on many modern writers and philosophers, including Herman Hesse, Christopher Isherwood, Aldus Huxley, J.D. Salinger and Henry Miller. We can only augment our knowledge and wisdom by utilizing this timeless wisdom.

Beyond the realm of body and mind, Eastern philosophy references the realm of spirit and soul. Christ, himself a man of the Middle East, said, "The Kingdom of Heaven is within." It was this kingdom that he advocated realizing and attaining above all else. It is at this point that many flee society and responsibility to seek truth or happiness in solitude and through the denial of day-to-day life. Yet, as Mahatma Gandhi, a great philosopher and world transformer said,

> *If I could persuade myself that I should find God in a Himalayan cave, I would proceed there immediately. But I know that I cannot find him apart from humanity.*[4]

It is from this vein of Eastern philosophy that we begin this journey. We must accept and live in this world, yet achieve or change things so as to increase both ours and the world's happiness and well being. We all ultimately seek only one thing: happiness. This takes many forms for many people. The role of this book is not to dictate and proclaim this or that as the true form of happiness, but rather to offer the reader a means of attaining his or her personal form of happiness.

The concept of intuition and one's heart-felt feeling play an important role in any spiritual quest. The mind, although a powerful use of our intelligence, is not the final step in mankind's evolution. Einstein attributed many of his discoveries to moments of insight and intuition. We must learn to acknowledge and trust our feelings when seeking our goals.

This book may introduce a few terms that are new to the reader, yet they will prove extremely helpful for our grasp of new ideas and ways of seeing our potential. Eastern philosophers often divide man into five aspects: body, vital, mind, heart, and soul.

The body is our physical existence.

The vital is our storehouse of earthbound energy, passion, and emotion that sustains our earthy existence. Vital energy encompasses everything from enthusiasm, excitement, and passion to frustration and anger.

Our mind, which is often mistakenly considered the pinnacle of our capacities, is the ability of thought, our thinking process. Beyond the realm of mind is our spiritual heart. The heart is that aspect of ourselves which embodies the qualities of love, oneness, and compassion. The heart though is not invincible. Even when aware of that part of ourselves, we can still fall under the influences of insecurity and self-doubt, which are generated in the mind and vital.

Beyond the realm of the heart is the soul. The soul is our direct connection with God, or as Sri Chinmoy says, "The Supreme." The soul is a spark of the eternal within us, undying and immortal. A conscious communion with this aspect of ourselves is the essence of all spiritual quests. Jesus taught, "The kingdom of heaven is within." This heaven is our soul, the spark of the eternal within our beings. In Eastern philosophy the terms "self-realization" and "God-realization" are used interchangeably to describe the state of being of one who has achieved this ecstacy with the eternal. This awareness is surely not the monopoly of the East and has been described by many Western mystics including St. Augustine, St. John, of the Cross, and Theresa of Avila.

Truly spiritual men and women use the word God, not to expound their particular conception or ideal of God, but to encompass the beliefs and ideals of all humanity. God has infinite attributes including Power, Peace, Joy and Satisfaction. Every man and woman is capable of realizing their oneness with the source of all creation.

"Aspiration" is another term that will be used in this writing. It means one's effort towards a spiritual goal. "Desire" is one's effort towards worldly pursuits. For example: Her desire was for fame and fortune, her aspiration was for oneness and humility. This differentiation is made not to create a vocabulary of spiritual elitism but to create a vernacular that distinguishes between mankind's myriad range of desires. The Eskimo language contains twenty-four words to describe snow. They know snow. It will help us in our understanding to differentiate between desire and aspiration. Desire is our movement to satisfy our ego and sense of separate self. Aspiration is our yearning for an awareness of our soul and a connectedness with humanity and life. We will also distinguish between success, as an outer achievement, and progress, as an inner achievement.

By placing the profound depths of Eastern philosophy within the framework of Western thought, analysis and organization, we will develop and cultivate a system that will help us to achieve all of our goals and life desires in a safe and harmonious manner. In a combination of the beat from East and West, we will find a unification of spirit and matter, science and spirituality.

Let us begin our journey towards success and progress with open hearts and minds, for as Mr. Hill noted more than half a century ago, "There are no limitations to the mind except those we acknowledge."

Sri Chinmoy writes: "It is a true truth that life was fast asleep in matter, and mind was fast asleep in life; now without the least hesitation we can say that something lies fast asleep in mind. The wheel of evolution ever moves — it stops not."[5] That which lies asleep in mind is our untapped and unknown potential. A potential and realm of possibility we will now unleash.

2

The Process

The ideas, theories and methodologies for the attainment of one's goals can be grouped into one of two basic methods: indomitable determination or absolute surrender. The West prefers the former, the East the latter.

Oftentimes the methodology of the East is vague when we try to find out exactly how to attain our goals. We are offered various mythologies and philosophical systems from which we are taught to discern both our greatness and smallness. Most Westerners relish the ideas espoused by Eastern philosophy, such as oneness with God, Nirvana, heaven, and other exalted states of awareness, yet have difficulty constructing a clear sense of how to attain these goals. Mahatma Gandhi, who was not only the leader of India's movement for independence, but also a deeply spiritual and moral man, summed up the conceptual framework espoused in Eastern philosophy:

> *I do dimly perceive that while everything around me is changing, ever dying, there is underlying all this change a living power that is changeless, that holds all together, that creates, dissolves and re-creates. That informing power or spirit is God.* [1]

The Eastern philosophy then most often prescribes an intuitive approach to that deeper awareness. Sarvepalli Radhakrishnan, one of India's most well-known contemporary philosophers states: "The rationality of the world is transparent to the intellect, but its mysteriousness can be grasped only by intuition."[2] In his own effort to unite East and West, he would later write:

> *Intuition is not independent but emphatically dependent upon thought and is immanent in the very nature of our thinking. It is dynamically continuous with thought and pierces through the conceptual content of knowledge to the living reality under it.*[3]

The process to attain our goals as outlined by Western thinkers is often clearer and much closer to the reasoning and scientific method espoused in our educational systems. We will use this type of clear, definitive system to create a framework for our journey. Although Western in nature, it will serve as a reservoir for Eastern ideas. We will follow a simple yet effective formula for success and attainment of goals:

1. Choose a goal.
2. Develop a plan of action.
3. Create a positive environment to work in.
4. Create a positive outlook: eliminate negative mental constructs.
5. Cultivate indomitable willpower.
6. Visualize and see the goal attained.
7. Act unceasingly until the goal is realized.

The ensuring chapters will describe in detail each of these steps.

To check this model, let's choose a simple goal: say, picking up a pen or pencil, anything small and near the hand. Watch your hand and the process at work. Identify each aspect in your experience.

First you choose your goal: to pick up the pencil. You develop a basic plan of how you will reach over and pick it up. You have already created a positive environment in that the pencil is in front of you and no one is threatening to stop you. The positive outlook is already in your possession. You know and feel you can accomplish your task. Indomitable willpower resides in the knowledge and belief that you can pick it up. You have a clear "vision" of how you will pick it up. Finally, you act.

Many of these elements, such as maintaining a positive outlook and eliminating negative mental ideas we take for granted when performing a simple act. We *know* we can pick up the pencil. Anyone would be hard pressed to convince us otherwise, yet "knowing" we can do it is essential to the process.

As we perceive tasks in life becoming more difficult our confidence begins to wane; we no longer *know* we can do something. Absolute confidence begins to be replaced by confidence tinged with doubt. If we still accomplish our goals we say "chance" and "luck" were on our side. When doubt becomes stronger than confidence we no longer accomplish our goals. We begin to "fail" and, mistakenly, take that as a reflection of our inadequacy as individuals. This is often followed by one of the greatest mistakes we can make: we go so far as to perceive ourselves not as the experiencers of failure, but as failures ourselves. We allow a few unfortunate thoughts to create for ourselves an identity as failures. This attitude is fatal and is addressed in detail in chapter 4.

Belief is essential to our success. Not necessarily a belief that we will always get what we desire, but a belief in ourselves and our sense of purpose. That which emerges when belief is gone, self-doubt, is one of the greatest stumbling blocks on the road to success and progress.

This seven step plan appears quite simple, yet the realization and practice of this method requires discipline and perseverance, especially during steps three through seven. As our goals expand so does the challenge to complete the final six steps. We will need a source of strength and encouragement from which we can cultivate the powerful discipline and perseverance. This strength, besides being necessitated by outer circumstances, will flow from an awareness of a spiritual aspect in our lives. We are more than just flesh and bones.

Eastern philosophy defines and expresses this realm of spirit and inspired energy far better than the Western scientists. In the West we often seek God, or truth, inside science and technology. God, or perfection, then becomes limited to a mental state. God exists at a far deeper level than our day-to-day mind can perceive. Eastern philosophy will take us to an understanding of this realm far more quickly than Western ideas. Let us be wise and travel the road which will bring us to our destination as soon as possible. Time is of the essence. We must re-connect with our inner, spiritual, and eternal self if we are to reach new heights and depths within ourselves and the world.

We will, therefore, combine the Western plan for success with the Eastern understanding of man's deep, inner nobility and immortality. The purpose of this book is *not* to espouse any particular belief system or philosophy, but rather to offer every reader the knowledge, tools, and inspiration to achieve whatever goals you have set for yourself.

Although this formula of seven steps has been presented in a sequential order, it is essential to understand that all aspects of this formula need to be used simultaneously. A plan without action is futile, action without determination is useless, determination overrun by self-doubt is sure frustration and disappointment, and a goal without a positive environment in which to pursue it is like swimming in shark-infested waters.

Review again the steps involved in the process of picking up the pencil. Try to see these seven steps in other tasks that you are able to accomplish. Understand that this is a working formula for success. It works when we apply all the steps. You unconsciously use this formula every day when performing simple tasks. We now want to take this same formula which we know works and apply it to goals we have not yet achieved. By seeing the formula in daily activities we will become familiar with it and this understanding will add to our confidence when applying the formula to greater tasks. We have a process that works. Let us now apply this formula to far-reaching, challenging goals.

EXERCISE 1

Review the seven steps again and commit them to memory. Identify these seven steps in at least three activities that you perform daily.

3

Choosing a Goal

The goals we choose dictate the direction of our lives. Without goals our life will have no direction. Our major life goals are closely linked with what we consider to be the purpose of our life. We need a sense of purpose to inspire us towards our goals and our goals will become the concrete manifestation of our feeling of purpose. This, then is our task: to develop a sense of purpose in our lives and to then choose goals based on that sense of purpose.

Some will argue at this point that life has no ultimate purpose and nothing we may do matters; life is meaningless.

We must each decide what is most important to us. If there are things we want to achieve and experience then we ought to adopt a philosophy that will strengthen our efforts. Life can be looked at from many directions. We need to choose a direction that will complement our personal effort. India's great poet and philosopher Rabindranath Tagore, a Nobel Prize winner, said it best: "The world appears to be an illusion only to those who approach it intellectually. It becomes positive and real to us when we enjoy it."[1]

One of the wonderful things about much of Eastern spiritual philosophy is the immense significance it gives to each life. Each individual, we are told, is in essence a microcosm of the entire universe. The only purpose of human life, it is taught, is to become consciously aware of that divinity within ourselves.

Sri Chinmoy writes:

Before taking human incarnation, the soul gets the inner message about its divine purpose on earth. It is fully conscious of its mission and it comes here with the direct approval or sanction of the Supreme. But during the lifetime, the workings of the physical mind sometimes cover up the divine inspiration of the soul and the true purpose of the soul. Then the mission of the soul cannot come forward. However, if we start aspiring with the mind, the heart and the soul, then we can learn the purpose of our existence here on earth.[2]

An understanding of our purpose in life is the first step towards choosing our major goals.

EXERCISE 2

Discovering the purpose of your life is no simple task. It requires much inner search and reflection. Set aside ten minutes for this exercise. Sit comfortably, away from distractions, and repeat to yourself over and over, silently or aloud, "What is the purpose of my life?" Concentrate as powerfully as possible on the repetition of this question. Do not search for an answer but rather allow the intensity of the question to lead you to an answer or feeling. Try this exercise a few times each week. An answer, feeling, new idea, or other inspiration will soon come to you clearing a new path of awareness in your life. Be patient but persistent.

We must spend time pondering and finding out what is most important to us and what we want to do for the world and ourselves. This understanding of ourselves will not come from watching television or reading the daily newspaper. To reach deeper aspects of ourselves, we need to directly experience our deeper nature.

This is done through periods of self-search as illustrated in the upcoming exercise.

We need to set aside time each day, or time every week, for self-reflection and meditation. We must give ourselves time and space in which to explore our deep thoughts and feelings. This does not need to be an elaborate, ceremonial event, but can simply be a quiet walk each evening, a solitary hike in the woods, or ten minutes of quiet time each day away from the distractions and pressures of everyday life. These moments of empowering aloneness will quickly become a wellspring of creativity and insight in our lives.

EXERCISE 3

Take a few minutes now to think about your life. Ask yourself, "What is the purpose of my life?" Ask this question over and over with all of your concentration until the very power of your search begins to resonate an answer from the depths of your being. The purpose is there, within each one of us, we only need to seek its voice in our hearts.

During these periods of quiet, our minds will drift from thought to thought, a plethora of emotions will drift through our consciousness. In these periods of reflection we need to address the deepest issues in our lives. Once we take care of the most important questions and issues the rest will fall into place or be seen from an entirely new perspective. Sri Chinmoy offers some advice on this topic:

If you have millions of questions about God and about yourself, you will be able to get most adequate answers to all of them by getting the proper answer to this one question: 'Who am I?' All the other questions revolve around this question. When you know the answer to this question, your life's problems are solved. Illumining questions, questions that come from the very depth of our heart concerning our inner progress and inner achievements, our self-realisation or God-realisation, are very few in number. Besides asking, 'Who am I?' you may want to know the answer to the question, 'What am I here for?' You may also have various specific questions about your own spiritual progress, which are bound to come to you spontaneously. But the only really important question is, 'Who am I?'[3]

The question, "Who am I?" will be answered little by little through our self-reflection. Each increment of increased awareness will bring us not only mental understanding but also a tremendous feeling of elation as we get closer and closer to the source of our existence. As we begin to inwardly explore and understand ourselves, we will get a strong feeling for the purpose of our life and the life goals that will naturally extend from that purpose. Our goals may change as we begin to understand ourselves more fully. These changes are not to be feared, but rather welcomed, as they reflect a deeper and more fulfilling sense of self and purpose.

Our goals do not have to be world-transforming; they can be simple and humble. Our goals can encompass both material and spiritual wealth. The essential factor in this process is that our goals emerge from within ourselves — from within our own minds and hearts. We need to cast aside the limiting ideas of contemporary society and those things which others think and tell us we should do. We must learn to follow the unique dreams each one of us has. One day we will realize the wonderful opportunity that life is. Sri Chinmoy writes:

If we discover the secret of speaking to our inner being, we will solve all our problems and discover the true meaning of our human ex-

istence. This human existence is a golden opportunity that the Supreme has granted us. We say that we don't have an opportunity; it is a sheer lie. The Supreme has given us the opportunity, but we do not avail ourselves of that opportunity.[4]

This "opportunity" is the ability to become conscious of ourselves and the purpose of our life. We must set aside the time, as mentioned earlier, for self-reflection. If we do not, we will merely bounce superficially through life as spectators, but not participants, in this great moment of living.

In choosing our goals we need to take into account that we are not one-dimensional beings. We have physical, material, emotional, and spiritual needs, desires, and aspirations. It is important that we take all of these into account when contemplating our lives. We need to understand the multi-dimensionality of our lives and give importance to each aspect.

By choosing material, physical, emotional, and spiritual goals we can create a healthy balance in our lives. The great psychologist Abraham Maslow spoke of a "hierarchy of needs" that must be fulfilled before man can ascend to "peak experiences."[5] This "hierarchy of needs" includes food, shelter and companionship. "Peak experiences" are described as moments of awareness and fulfillment far transcending our day-to-day consciousness.

Many cultures have given great importance to these "peak" or spiritual experiences. Unfortunately, in our Western society, dominated by dogmatic Christian philosophy, direct experience of God or Truth is not stressed as a possibility. In our society the concept of spiritual awakening is reserved for a select few and awaits the masses only upon death. This view is not in line with the original teachings of Jesus Christ who taught that we must all seek the kingdom of heaven within ourselves, here and now.

These spiritual moments of awakening can be felt by everyone. All we need to do is to give some time and importance to this aspect of our lives. For this reason we need to create goals for ourselves in both the physical and spiritual realm. The world, in general, and most societies, lack this balance; but if we can create this equilibrium in our own lives it will have a more powerful effect than we can imagine.

It is in this same way that we need to unite the philosophies of East and West. The West has abundant food and shelter but few "spiritual" or "peak experiences." The East professes centuries of "spiritual discovery" yet often cannot feed or clothe her masses. If we can unite these two, we will create for ourselves a true sense of life and self, valuing both our physical and spiritual aspects.

The following two exercises are essential. Give yourself plenty of time to work through them. Your goals are the foundation of your life. These exercises will help you explore your goals and integrate them into your day-to-day life.

EXERCISE 4

On a piece of paper write down the following categories: physical, financial, emotional, and spiritual. Next to each of these write, in a sentence or two, your general sense of purpose for each category. For example, next to emotional you may write: "To create and give importance to relationships that are fulfilling and healthy." Take your time doing this. You may find yourself changing your purpose as you think more deeply about each subject.

The "physical" category deals with your body and health. "Financial" encompasses your material wants and needs. The "emotional" category will deal with friendships, relationships, and your interaction with other human beings. The category of "spiritual" addresses your deepest feelings regarding the purpose of your life and the need to explore those feelings.

These general statements of purpose should be the expression of your deep feelings about your life and exactly where you want it to go.

Now, below each category, write one or two goals you have for that aspect of your life. These should support the earlier statement of purpose. For example, under "physical" your purpose may have been, "to create and maintain a healthy body through exercise and nutrition." Now the specific goals can be:

1. To exercise for at least ten minutes every day.

2. To make sure you eat a healthy breakfast each day.

The goals you set will make or break this system. You need to set goals that are realistic and take into account where you are now. Make your goals "non-judgmental," in that the attainment of the goal is not based on an opinion or rigid standard. This is exemplified by the difference between the goals: "I will exercise ten minutes a day" and "I want to look trim and be beautiful." The first goal is an action-related goal. The second is based on the opinions of yourself or others and is far too prone to fluctuations.

Goal setting is a skill and an art. We always have the ability to act, but not always to influence what results will occur. Set your goals as action-oriented.

For example, let's say your sense of purpose in the "emotional" category is to 'create and give importance to relationships that are productive and healthy.' An excellent action-related goal for this category would be: 'I will be kind and outgoing to all new people I meet.' This is an action we can perform that will have positive effects in ways we cannot even imagine. A goal that would be unproductive or out of our control would be, "to be liked by all new people I meet" or "to become good friends with new people I meet." These last two goals depend on situations and feelings you cannot control. What if the next three people you meet never like anybody they meet for the first time? All you can do is be kind and outgoing. You are not in control of other people's feelings.

This principle should apply to all of your goals. You can eat well and exercise, but you cannot consciously cause your body to weigh less than it does now. This will most likely occur, but center your goals on what you can control.

Let's say that under 'spiritual' your purpose is to give people hope and joy in their lives through your guitar music. One of your general goals that you want to accomplish is to improve your guitar playing. Action-oriented goals would be to "practice one hour every day" or "take two lessons each week." These are excellent goals. Unproductive goals would be to 'become a great guitarist' or 'become as good as so and so.' What if so and so keeps getting better, faster than you do? You will never reach your goal and get frustrated. Soon you will find yourself wishing for their demise so you can surpass them! By choosing action goals we assure that we are the masters of our destiny.

We do not want to compare ourselves to others so much, but rather seek to explore and express the best within ourselves. We each have something unique to offer to the world. If we always imitate others we will only create imitations and never originals.

Our goals need to be attainable and within your view of possibility, yet far-reaching enough to challenge and inspire you. Your goals should give you a sense of excitement and hopefulness. Choose goals that are challenging, yet realistic. These goals are not set in stone. As you achieve each goal, you set new ones. Your ability to create attainable, challenging goals is one of the first keys to your success.

EXERCISE 5

The following is a very challenging exercise. You will need to have all of your goals and purposes written down and in front of you. If you have not done so already, put them down in writing.

Now, the challenging part: see if for an entire day everything you do can be directed towards one of your goals. This can be a very powerful experience. It also tests that your goals are not too limiting. You should have goals that are general enough and inspiring enough so that each day, in one way or another, you are working at each moment towards your goals. You will quickly see when you are "wasting time" and when you are moving in the life direction you have chosen.

Choose certain days to be 'goal only' days. These days will be your most fulfilling and you will want to have more and more of them. Again, don't be too rigid in your thinking or goal setting. The goals of "getting healthy" and "improving friendships" could both be encompassed by a day on the beach, swimming, and enjoying fresh air and sun with some friends. By being conscious of our goals at all times, we can empower our mundane day-to-day experiences with a deep relevance and significance.

4

Developing a Plan

Once we have carefully chosen our goals we need to develop a plan to acquire that which we desire.

We are trying to create and achieve something and a plan will assure that our energy will be focused towards our goals. There are different types of planning and plans. We know what we are and possess and we know what we want to become and possess. Our plan is the link between what is and what we desire to be.

We can choose from different types of planning based on the type of person we are and the type of structure under which we work best.

The first type of planning entails figuring out each step we will take along the road to our goal.

It is similar to the blueprints for the construction of a building. We devise a plan and carry it out step by step. This type of planning works well when there are few variables that we have to deal with. Variables, though, invariably arise. We will often need to construct contingency plans in order to deal with these variables. If we are designing the plans for a house in the woods and we are not yet sure if a stream runs through the property during the winter; we may make two sets of plans, one encompassing the stream the other not.

As the possible number of variables begins to increase we find that we need to be more and more flexible and adaptable in our planning. This necessitates the need for spontaneity in our plans and actions.

To illustrate the need for solid, definite planning and spontaneity let us take the example of crossing a forest on a dark night. We clearly know our goal: to cross the forest. We have a compass and know the general direction we need to take. Once it is dark though, we can no longer see what is directly ahead of us and we need to adapt to an ever-changing situation. We keep our overall plan fixed in our mind yet we are constantly refining and adapting our plan based on the forest's unknown twists and changes.

Whoever or whatever was the unseen hand behind the creation of our universe, surely must have known a lot about planning. The intricacy and interdependence of nature is a creation far beyond the capacity of man's mind. We can begin to understand life in small aspects, but an understanding of the entire creation eludes us. Sri Chinmoy refers to this creative aspect as God. He writes:

We have a physical body and a mind. Similarly, we can think of God as a physical being, having a mind like ours. People often imagine God as composed of a gigantic mind, or else functioning like them with the mind. Up until now, the mind has been humanity's greatest achievement. With the help of the mind, science and our physical world have progressed to an enormous extent. As the mind has been our highest attainment, we tend to think of God as a being with a most highly developed mind. But God is not a mental being. God does not act from the mind. He does not need the mental formulations which we utilize in order to act. God does not need to formulate ideas in a mental way.

Human beings usually think before they act. But in God's case, it is not like that. He uses His Willpower which, while seeing, also acts and becomes. God's seeing, acting and becoming are simultaneous and instantaneous.[1]

Science, or mental investigation, can offer us only slight glimpses of the wonderment of creation. The immensity of creation can only be perceived through a deeper awareness than provided by the mind alone. Tagore wrote: "There is a stream of life within me. I experience it, and through it I also experience my oneness with the world around me."[2] When developing our own plans it is important to keep the immensity and beauty of nature's plan in our hearts. Nature is always in fluctuation. Creating a plan that allows for change as necessity demands it will help us towards our goals.

A flexible plan which takes into account the possibility of unknown obstacles or difficulties is quite different from a plan which admits to its abandonment if the going gets too tough. We must stay focused on our goal and move towards it as quickly as we are able to. Each time we stop or move backwards due to difficulties, self-doubt or any other unproductive idea or emotion, we are delaying the attainment of our goals.

The second type of planning is based on the idea of absolute spontaneity. We can fixate wholeheartedly upon our goal and step towards it with unwavering determination although we may have no specific plan. In other words, our plan can be one of complete trust in the importance of our goal and in our determination to always act towards that goal. Our plan then becomes not one of trying to anticipate the future, but rather acting always towards our goal and having a deep faith in that goal and in ourselves. With a deep faith in ourselves we can overcome any obstacle or difficulty as long as our attention is focused solidly on our goal. Without the double anchor of belief in ourselves and faith in our goal, we will not be able to weather the tumultuous storms, trials, and tribulations that we will surely face. How might the Creator plan the universe? Sri Chinmoy writes:

Right now we are labouring with our mind. The mind says, "I have to achieve something. I have to think about how I can execute my plan." But God does not do that. God sees the past, present and future at a glance. When we are one with God, when — by constant aspiration — we identify ourselves with God's Consciousness, then whatever we do will be done spontaneously. Then we will not utilize the mind, but always act from our own inner consciousness, with our intuitive faculty. And when we develop that intuitive faculty, we can easily act without having a plan. At each moment, the possibility of the total manifestation that is going to take place will materialize right in front of us.[3]

A plan is meaningless without a goal. A goal is a mere dream, or fantasy, without a plan. The loftier or more far-reaching the goal, the more profound the plan. Others may laugh at our goal and plan but we must not be deterred by their lack of vision.

Thomas Edison tried ten thousand experiments before the light bulb was created. Many must have thought him mad, yet he clearly had a goal, a plan, and determination.

Oftentimes the necessary plan will spontaneously emerge from the goal. We will, of course, have a goal before we have a plan. By focusing on our goal we will soon begin to develop a plan. This will happen in one of two ways. We will either consciously set about to gather information regarding the attainment of our goal or intuition will step in to play its role and a sense of plan will emerge from the goal. A combination of these two may also occur.

Within everything exists the essence of that from which it was created. The building blocks of the solar system exist within each atom. By carefully examining a chair, we can come to understand the mind and plan of the carpenter who created it.

The more we believe in and intensify our goals in our minds and lives, the more real they will become to us. As we come to know our goals more fully, we will intuitively begin to know that which went into its creation. The "plan" for its creation will be revealed to us in proportion to how well we visualize and create an awareness of our goal.

Imagine you are looking at a great work of art. You are seeing what had been the goal of the painter. You do not see the artist, studio, brushes or cans of paint; yet, upon careful observation of the goal, the painting, you can know the plan, the ways and means used to create the goal.

This is the reason that visualization and auto-suggestion work as means to attain goals. The more we can "see" something, the more real it becomes and hence the more the goal reveals to the observer how it was created. We then need only follow the plan revealed to us. It has been said that anything which we can imagine exists in some realm, and that is precisely why we can conceive of it.

Every plan must take into account the need for meditative and self-reflective time. We must create quiet times for ourselves during which we can re-energize our minds and hearts towards our goals. The difficulties and challenges of life will constantly distract us from our goals. We need, on a daily basis, to refocus ourselves towards that which is most important to us.

We are bombarded daily by an endless stream of influences from society, our families, friends, advertisers, and the media. If we are to stay in touch with our feelings, goals, and aspirations, we need to set aside time for us to solidify our goals. Spending a few minutes each day in meditation or quietly reflecting away from the distractions of daily life will harmonize our feelings and actions.

Let us choose far-reaching goals that express our true potential. By seeing, visualizing and believing in our goal we will create a reality that will reveal what will be necessary for its creation. To this we must add the acquisition of pertinent knowledge.

We must gather practical, concrete information about our goal which will help us in the formation of a plan. The more pertinent information we can acquire, the more variables and aspects we will be able to understand about our goal. The more we understand our goal, the more intelligent our plan will be.

Another method for gathering information is called "modeling." If you are in a situation, say the first year of law school, and are having a difficult time, look around and find people who are doing well. How are they managing? What is their attitude? Ask successful people about their plans and strategy and then model their behavior, plan, and attitude, always adapting it to suit you. By watching carefully to see who is succeeding and then asking them questions or observing them, we can see what is working. By then applying those strategies to our situation we will be immediately stepping into a successful strategy and saving ourselves countless hours, days and possibly years of trial-and-error efforts. Model and adopt success.

It has been said that knowledge is not power; the proper use of knowledge is power. By having a goal we are able to put into use and action all of the knowledge we acquire: both intuitive knowledge and factual, concrete knowledge. Through the application and use of this combined knowledge, we will surely reach our goals.

As we proceed towards the creation of our plans, let us keep in mind the words spoken by Swami Vivekananda at the turn of the century:

The secret of wisdom is to think: "I am the spirit, not the body, and the whole of this Universe, with all its relations, with all of its good and evil, is but a series of paintings — scenes on a canvas of which I am the witness."[4]

EXERCISE 6

Take one of your goals and visualize it. Make the image as colorful and real as possible. Try to feel the existence of that reality. What actions must be taken for you to bridge the gap between reality now and your goal? This is the beginning of your formulation of a plan. Write down what you need to do. Do this exercise once a day until you have a clear plan and feeling. Do you need more practical information to help you? Gather this information at school, public libraries, and any other sources of information available to you.

5

Creating a Positive Environment

It has been said that individual will is strong, but the environment is stronger. The people and ideas we surround ourselves with not only reflect who we are now but point to what we are likely to become. The people and ideas around us not only represent us, they greatly influence us.

One of the primary concepts of the Buddha's path to spiritual discipline was the concept of the "sangha" or the spiritual community of which one was a part. If we spend our time with thieves, we may well become a thief. If we spend our time with positive, dynamic, optimistic people, they and their thoughts and feelings are sure to rub off on us.

At the same time, if we spend our time with people who are constantly doubting themselves and seeing the worst in all situations, this will begin to affect our own attitude. If we truly value our goals then we must give tremendous importance to environment and time.

Once we have established goals for ourselves then we need to take a good look at reality. When we do this, we will clearly see that there are severe limitations in the human life. Time is one of them. We only have 60, 70, or 80 years to achieve that which we have put before us. When we value time we will do everything possible to expedite our pursuits. We will enhance our progress by associating with individuals and groups that value the same interests as us. It will be helpful if you can form a group of associates to help you work towards your goals. A philosopher once noted, "the sum is greater than any of its parts." By uniting with others who share our goals and aspirations we will increase our own capacity and inspiration. Sri Chinmoy offers another example:

In the spiritual life when you want to discipline your life, you have to mix with spiritual

*people who have disciplined their lives. You
are trying to discipline your life and they are
also in the same boat. So when two persons
are aiming at the same goal it makes the task
very easy. Early in the morning it is difficult
to run because of lethargy and inertia. But if
you see that a friend of yours is running, you
will go together. At that time, you will energize him and he will energize you. Your
strength enters into his strength and his
strength enters into your strength.*[1]

This same idea applies to that which we
choose to allow to enter our consciousness or
awareness from the outer environment. If we are
beginning to get an intimation, an inner feeling,
concerning the deep significance, beauty, and
purpose of our life, then going and reading an
essay on existential philosophy and man's ultimate purposelessness will not prove beneficial
to what you are trying to achieve. Not that this
nihilistic attitude is bad or incorrect, but once
you have chosen certain goals and life directions
you ought to do everything possible to inspire
yourself towards those ends.

The mind is a very delicate instrument. It believes almost everything put into it. Think back
to when you cried at a sad movie, or were scared
at a horror film; in the midst of the movie the
mind forgets true and false and just takes in in-

formation and feeds it to our body and emotional nature. Our thoughts create a reality as well. If you think the plane you're on is about to crash, fear will rush through your body. You will become nervous and frightened. That thought may have nothing to do with reality, but you react all the same. We need to safeguard ourselves from unproductive energy.

If we read depressing novels all the time, we will spend our time in a melancholic state. If every day we read apocalyptic prophecies of doom, we will be affected accordingly.

Once we begin to understand the significance of what we fill our minds with, there are two things we need to do. The first is to safeguard ourselves from useless and trivial information that merely distracts us from deeper thoughts and feelings. By eliminating the insignificant, we are able to spend more time and thought with that which is of greater importance to us.

The second thing we need to do is to constantly inspire ourselves towards our goal. This can involve reading encouraging accounts of those who have succeeded in their goals. It also entails surrounding ourselves with others who will encourage us and believe in the same things we do. No one exists without interaction with the environment, whether that environment means books, people, ideas or nature. If you wish to succeed in business, read stories of great industrial and business leaders and feel the determination and power of those who have achieved. Fill yourself with the belief that you can, like them, succeed. Don't go to bankruptcy court and surround yourself with the thoughts and emotions of those who have failed. That would only serve to discourage you and bring into your consciousness the fear that you, yourself, may end up there.

Swami Vivekananda addressed this issue nearly a century ago:

> *If a man, day and night, thinks he is miserable, low, and nothing, nothing he becomes. If you say, "Yea, yea, I am, I am," so shall you be; and if you say, "I am not," think that you are not, and day and night meditate upon the fact that you are nothing, ay, nothing shall you be. That is the great fact which you ought to remember. We are the children of the Almighty; we are sparks of the infinite Divine Fire. How can you be nothing? We are everything, we can do everything—and man must do everything.*[2]

Assuredly, we do not want to delude ourselves into the realm of fantasy by filling our minds with unfounded facts. This will be avoided if we have searched our souls when seeking our goals.

If our goals are pure and sound, then their attainment will be safe and rewarding.

Another important factor towards our success is not only the people and ideas we surround ourselves with, but also the memories that we hold onto in our lives. Letting go of past negative experiences, resolving them and going forward, is one of the great keys to success. The person carrying the least weight can run the fastest.

This idea of letting go applies to fears, failures, bad experiences, moments of insecurity and many other so-called negative experiences. An excellent illustration of this can be found in Sri Chinmoy's suggestions regarding guilt, that lingering emotion which cripples so many of us.

You should feel that the past is buried in oblivion. If you cherish the idea of guilt when you have done something wrong, you are being sincere, but this act of mere sincerity, does not help. Yes, you have done something wrong, but by thinking of your mistake and having a guilty consciousness, you do not get light or wisdom. Suppose you have done something that is not right. So from now on, you will try to do the right thing, the divine thing. This minute you have used for a wrong purpose. Then use the following minute for a divine purpose. If you do this without think-

*ing of the previous minute when you did
something wrong, then what happens? Your
positive strength, this willpower you have
used to do the right thing, will have all its
power. But if you think of the past minute
with a sense of guilt while you are doing the
right thing now, then half your power is again
lost in darkness and only half can be utilized
for the right action.*

*If you cherish or brood over your misdeeds,
then you are strengthening your guilt unconsciously. You should feel, "If I have done something wrong, I am ready to face it. If I have
done something wrong, then I have the capacity to do the thing right." By focusing all
attention on the right thing, you are adding
to your positive strength.*

*The sense of guilt, the constant feeling of
self-reproach is, unfortunately, all-pervading
in the Western world. If my source is God, the
absolute infinite Light, then some day I must
go back to my Source. During my stay on
earth, I got unfortunately some unhealthy,
unaspiring and destructive experiences. Now
I have to get rid of these unfortunate experiences in my life. And for that I have to concentrate only on the right things, the divine
things which will fulfill me, and not on the
things that have stood in my way.*[3]

The attainment of our goals will be swift and sure if we can surround ourselves with those who share common ideas, aspirations, goals and feelings. We must allow into our consciousness only that which moves us emotionally and intellectually towards our desires. We need to discover and cultivate the powers and abilities within ourselves that we all possess. This strength and potentiality is often veiled from us, yet those who know the true potentials of man point us towards our inner strengths. Swami Vivekananda said:

All the strength and succour you want is within yourselves. Therefore make your own future. Let the dead past bury its dead. The infinite future is before you, and you must always remember that each word, thought, and deed lays up a store for you, and that as the bad thoughts and bad deeds are ready to spring upon you like tigers, so also there is the inspiring hope that the good thoughts and good deeds are ready, with the power of a hundred thousand angels, to defend you always and forever.[4]

If we take the time and effort to cultivate the trees of our potential, the fruits and flowers which will grow will be far beyond our own imaginations. With the proper environment for growth the power of a "hundred thousand angels" will be quite a help as we reach towards our goals.

EXERCISE 7

Figure out how much time each week you spend subjecting yourself to information that is irrelevant to your life goals. Write down the figure in hours per week. How could you use this time more productively towards the attainment of your goals? Most Americans average four hours of television per day. That's almost thirty hours a week!

Now write down the names of the five people you voluntarily spend most of your time with. Are these people helping you attain your goals? Can they start doing something to help you? What kind of people would most help you towards your goals? If you don't already know these people how can you meet them?

6

Eliminating Negative Thoughts and Conceptions

The previous chapter touched briefly on the central theme of this chapter: if we are to move forward swiftly in life towards our goals we need to lighten the amount of negative mental baggage we carry with us. Negative thoughts, such as fear, and negative conceptions, such as failure, will cause us to move more slowly towards our goals. The elimination of these will assure our progress.

Memories of failure are often the strongest memories we carry with us. This is because of the intense emotions that accompany moments of supposed failure. Rejection, embarrassment, humiliation, and fear often walk hand in hand with feelings of failure.

One of the ways to eliminate these types of thoughts, emotions, and memories is to rework our conception of certain types of experience. The intense emotion that accompanied the experience will be there regardless of how you label the emotion and the experience. If you've worked hard at something, there will be intense feelings and emotions accompanying any result. Because we label the result as "failure" we have a strong negative experience and consequent memory. What if we had labeled the result as a "powerful learning experience" instead? Then, armed with the same outpouring of invested emotion we would have the positive emotion and memory of a "powerful learning experience." The energy of the experience will be well imbedded for future reference. Instead of a failure experience we would have a learning experience. We would then have an invaluable tool for continued learning, rather than a feeling of failure, rejection, and embarrassment. By reworking our conception we move from a negative experience to a learning experience. Why

not replace success and failure with the all-encompassing idea of learning?
The fear of failure is one of our greatest fears. The memory of failure can be debilitating in our life. Sri Chinmoy addresses this issue of fear:

You have to know what failure is and what failure can do. Fear is bound to go when you know that failure is not something shameful, damaging, destructive or painful. Feel that failure is something natural. When a child starts to walk, he often stumbles and falls down. But the moment he knows how to walk, he does not feel that stumbling was a failure. He thinks that it was a natural process to stand up for a moment and then fall again.

If you think of failure in that light, not as something that is against or totally distant from reality but as something that is forming, shaping, molding and becoming reality, then there cannot be any fear. We take failure as something contrary to our expectation and our God-realisation. But failure is not contrary to our realization. Failure is something that is urging us to our own realization. For what we call failure, in God's Eye, is only an experience.

Always take failure as an experience. Do not take it as a finished product or as the cul-

mination of an experience, but rather as the process of an experience. If you think that failure is the end of your experience, then you are mistaken. In a long race one may start very slowly, but then gradually he increases his speed and eventually he reaches his goal. But if he thinks that since his start was slow, he will not be able to reach the destination, then he is making a deplorable mistake. If there is no failure, naturally you will run the fastest. But if there is failure, take it as an experience that is just beginning. The end is the success. And then who can say that you have failed? Who is the judge? If you are the judge, then no matter what you do and what you achieve, you will always feel that you have failed. But if somebody else is the judge, then he will know whether your so-called failure is real. He will call your experience a failure only when you do not want to overcome what you feel is wrong within you. When you give up the spiritual life, that is failure. Otherwise, there is no such thing in my terminology as failure.[1]

By reworking our conceptions and attitudes regarding various situations we can drastically alter their effect on us. Nervousness can easily be transformed into excitement, fear into preparedness and insecurity into self-knowledge. Let's take nervousness as an example.

I know a certain well-known public speaker who says that when she was first beginning to speak publicly she used to get so nervous she couldn't sit still; her mind would race and her stomach feel queasy. That was when she was quite unsure of her abilities. Now, many years later, she knows she is a talented, well-admired speaker. These days, before she speaks, she describes a wonderful rush of energy through her entire body, her mind runs through all points of her speech with amazing speed and accuracy and she gets a feeling of power and excitement in her stomach. Guess what? She said it's the same essential feeling as fifteen years ago. The emotions and feelings have not changed, only her relation to them, her conception of them, and how she uses the energy created in that moment.

We can replace the idea of failure with the idea of learning. We can also change and replace the connotations and hence implications we give to certain feelings and emotions. The next time you get that "feeling" in your stomach call it excitement instead of nervousness. Say out loud, "I'm excited" instead of "I'm nervous." You'll be amazed at the difference.

Replace those ideas of jealousy and insecurity with the necessity for a deeper understanding of your true self-worth, of what it is that makes you who you are. Replace the ideas of loneliness and boredom with the quest for greater self-understanding. Life is short and the moments few. Use them to the fullest. Seize the opportunity in every moment. Replace frustration with a determination to change things that make you unhappy. Muster up all your dissatisfactions in life and cultivate that energy into a cyclone for change. There is no time to waste. Value your goal. The energy necessary for success is at hand. The following poem by Sri Chinmoy expresses the power of negative thoughts and emotions:

No Little Enemy
There is no little enemy.
A wee fear
Tortures our whole existence.
A tiny doubt
Devours our entire being.
A puny jealousy
Destroys our universal oneness.

The anecdote to fear is surely courage. The way to attain that courage is to allow your consciousness and awareness to expand into a feeling of connectedness with all of life. When we feel that something is part and parcel of us then we do not fear it. We do not fear our hands, or friends, or the things we know to be ours.

Fear is another powerful force which prevents individuals from finding their true potential. We fear many things: from death to earthquakes, most of which we have no control over. Anytime that we try to expand the scope of our lives, try new things, or express new capacities, we will surely find fear knocking at our door. Fear will try to hold us back from that which we seek to know or express. Why? Sri Chinmoy:

The thing that holds you back is fear, which has no meaning at all. If you want the wealth which the ocean holds deep inside itself, then you have to dive within. Fear and wealth don't go together. Only if you have inner courage can you receive the inner wealth. It is fear of the unknown and the unknowable that prevents you from diving deep within. But what is unknowable today becomes merely unknown tomorrow, and the day after tomorrow it becomes known. The vastness of Truth will never destroy you. It will only embrace and fulfill you.

You feel afraid of something because you do not feel that that particular thing is part of you. But through meditation you establish your conscious oneness with the infinite Vast. At that time you see that everything is part of you. So how can you be afraid?[2]

Fear has existed in man since the beginning of creation, yet it can be overcome and transcended. Courage and faith are essential to conquer fear. Swami Vivekananda wrote:

Be not afraid of anything. You will do marvelous work. The moment you fear, you are nobody. It is fear that is the great cause of misery in the world. It is fear that is the greatest of superstitions. It is fear that is the cause of our woes. And it is fearlessness that brings heaven in a moment.

The only religion that ought to be taught is the religion of fearlessness. Either in this world or in the world of religion, it is true that fear is the sure cause of degradation and sin. It is fear that brings misery, fear that brings death, fear that breeds evil. And what causes fear? Ignorance of our own nature.[3]

EXERCISE 8

Here are two practical things you can do to eliminate negative thoughts and emotions. First, don't think in terms of failure and success. This type of thinking will strangle you. Think only in terms of action. Act as powerfully as you can and then objectively watch the results. Assess the new situation and then act once more. We have the power to act, but the results are often beyond our ability to control; therefore, don't dwell on the results as a reflection of your worth as a person. Dwelling on failure will destroy us. Dwelling too much on success will make us overly proud and often complacent. Act to your capacity and then offer up the results of your action to experience and learning.

The second technique, which is effective and empowering, is to not label the emotions you feel, or, if necessary, to label them in a positive way. Reread the example from this chapter of the woman speaker. Label your emotions as excitement instead of nervousness; heightened awareness instead of anxiety; and the need for change instead of frustration. This reworking of your conceptions is not difficult, yet it is unbelievably powerful. The emotion of frustration is immediately followed by the feeling of helplessness. But if we change frustration into the feeling of needing a change, then this new emotion will be followed by the necessity for action. The decision is yours. Would you rather be crippled by a feeling of hopelessness or enlivened by a feeling of the need for powerful action? The difference depends only on how you conceptualize the very same emotion.

This very same technique can be used for any debilitating emotion you experience. Simply use the formulas given in the two examples in this exercise. You can also use these ideas to rework your memory of past experiences. Turn all those negative memories of failure into memories of experience and learning.

7

Cultivating Indomitable Willpower

If your life is devoid of resolve
You will not be able to solve
Any problem that you encounter.

— SRI CHINMOY

That which man can think and believe he can assuredly achieve. As we replace our negative mind-sets with positive ones we will radically change the perception of our experiences. As these negative thoughts and ideas begin to diminish we will act more often and more powerfully. Our action — both mental and physical — towards our goals will be ceaseless and unstoppable. We have learned how to clear away our self-created inner boundaries to success and progress.

As you begin to straighten up your mind and emotions you will become aware of one of the most powerful forces known to man: human willpower. When a person stands determined, undaunted by fear and doubt, that person is in the realm of pure will.

Willpower is a state of being that lies at the core of our consciousness. It is a state of being that can, and has, moved mountains and nations. When our willpower is joined with a positive and world-helping goal, then our force will be doubled. If our willpower is joined with questionable activities, then the result may be an unfortunate experience.

Sri Chinmoy links courage and willpower as different manifestations of the same energy:

Courage is our inner indomitable will. The outer expression of our inner indomitable will is manifested in the form of outer courage. Each moment we can see the reality, stand in front of the reality and grow into the reality if our existence is inundated with the inner will and the outer courage.[1]

This willpower and courage will be the natural outcome of our process if we take each step along the way carefully. Let's review the process so far. Firstly, we have considered our lives deeply and chosen our goals. Then we foster a positive environment where our ideas and aspiration can grow and flourish. We then eliminate negative mind sets and preconceptions, replacing these with productive ideas and emotions. Once these steps are taken we will find a new power dawning in our lives. This power is our spirit's will and determination.

Through determination and will our goals and desires are brought into reality. Sri Chinmoy has written: "When my inner will energizes my outer existence, all my imponderable troubles and excruciating pangs dissolve into thin air."[2]

Our power to plan and act comes from our strong desire to attain our goals. If our goals are linked to our deeper purposes in life then our power and determination will come from our own depths, what many spiritual teachers term the soul.

Again, Sri Chinmoy:

Determination ultimately comes from the soul. When we use this power on the physical, vital, or mental plane — that is to say, on the outer plane — we call it determination. But when we use it on the inner or psychic plane, we call it willpower, the light of the soul. 'Willpower' is the spiritual term that we use for determination. When the light of the soul enters into the vital, we can have one-pointed determination. This one-pointed determination is divine determination, real willpower.

In ordinary human life, when we are determined to do something, we maintain our determination for five minutes and then all our determination is gone. If we try to achieve determination on our own, it will not last. But once we know what the soul's willpower is, we see that it lasts for many years, even for a lifetime.[3]

In order to assure that our determination, concentration and willpower are coming from our soul, we need to once again make sure that our goals are resonating from the depths of our being. If our goals and desires stem from a deep inner search then our soul's spirit and determination will come to the fore to guide us towards our destination. Conversely, if we have not laid a solid foundation in the choice of our goals we may find ourselves coming up short on determination and willpower when it comes time for us to act, or after we have faced formidable setbacks.

Patience plays an important role in our cultivation of determination and willpower. Patience is the power and force to continue in the face of difficulty. Even when we do not immediately get that which we seek, patience will prevent us from giving up. Sri Chinmoy writes:

If failure has the strength to turn your life into bitterness itself, then patience has the strength to turn your life into the sweetest joy. Do not surrender to fate after a single failure. Failure, at most, precedes success. But success once achieved, confidence becomes your name.[4]

Patience and determination go hand in hand. Determination without patience quickly leads to frustration. Determination coupled with patience assures our success. Patience allows us to step back and watch our actions take form. Rome was not built in a day. Nor will our goals appear overnight. It takes time for things to happen and patience is our knowledge of that simple fact: change takes time.

Each step forward towards our goals and each step forward towards determination and unstoppable willpower are one and the same. Our ability to face challenges will be intensified if we can stay focused on our aim. Patience, courage, determination, and willpower will assure that we will not cease to go forward until the goal is reached.

Our willpower and sense of determination will naturally emerge as we solidify the importance of our goal and eliminate negative mind sets. Think of determination as your natural state of being that is now eclipsed by unproductive thoughts and emotions. Remove or transform those thoughts and willpower will be yours. As the sun cannot forever remain hidden by clouds, so too your inner power will not always remain obscured by thought.

Once you have accessed willpower and determination in your life, you will achieve abilities and experiences you never imagined could be yours. Once we know our goal to be all important to us, we will do all that is necessary to achieve our goal. That action is our determination and willpower.

As we begin to move towards our goals with determination, we will learn to develop faith in ourselves and in our abilities. Swami Vivekananda noted,

Throughout the history of mankind, if any one motive power has been more potent than others in the lives of great men and women, it is that of faith in themselves. Born with the consciousness that they were to be great, they became great.[5]

Unfortunately most of us are not born with this mindset. We are given a different view of ourselves. Swami Vivekananda notes these but then offers us a great challenge:

Men are taught from childhood that they are weak and that they are sinners. Teach them that they are all glorious children of immortality, even those who are the weakest in manifestation. Let positive, helpful thoughts enter into their brains from their very childhood. Lay yourself open to these thoughts, and not to weakening and paralysing ones. Say to your own mind, "I am He, I am He." Let it ring day and night in your minds like a song, and at the point of death declare, "I am He." That is the truth. The infinite strength of the world is yours.

Do you know how much energy, how many powers, how many forces, are still lurking behind that frame of yours? What scientist has known all that is in man? Millions of years have passed since man came here, and yet but one infinitesimal part of his powers has been manifested. Therefore you must not say that you are weak. How do you know what possibilities lie behind that degradation on the surface? You know but little of that which is within you; for behind you is the ocean of infinite power and blessedness.[6]

Self-doubt is one of the greatest stumbling blocks we will face on the road to progress, success, and willpower. Self-doubt cripples our inner march. All too often we doubt ourselves, our goals and our abilities. We all have shortcomings, but the awareness of our lack of perfection does not need to lead to self-doubt. Our failures do not need to lead to self-doubt. Mahatma Gandhi, the great Indian philosopher and political leader, offers a unique perspective: "To find truth completely is to realize oneself and one's destiny, that is, to become perfect. I am painfully conscious of my imperfections, and therein lies all the strength that I possess."[7]

Rather than harboring self-doubt and allowing that feeling to smother your life, admit your shortcomings and take definite steps towards improving those skills which you lack. At the same time pride yourself on your strengths and use them as powerfully and as often as possible. No two people are the same. We all have different strengths and weaknesses. Don't compare yourself to others — it is a waste of time. We all need to expand our individual capacities, then only can all of human kind walk together towards perfection.

8

Visualization

In the chapter on developing a plan, we explored the role of visualization in the manifestation of our goal. Here we will develop a deeper understanding of the process of visualization and why it works.

Every success formula or attempt to understand the condition of man gives great importance to the ideas, beliefs, and images which people hold in their minds. "As you think, so shall you become," has been uttered by prophets, teachers, and philosophers since recorded history began. Christ himself stressed over and over the role of "faith" and "belief" in the attainment of Heaven. The thoughts, ideas, and feelings we carry with us are a tremendous power.

Along with the cultivation of determination, willpower, courage, and other qualities, we must learn to visualize our goals. By fostering images of our goals we actually conceive, or give birth to, that reality.

It is well documented that visualization techniques work in the attainment of goals. By visualizing their ideal performance, many athletes have improved their performance. With physical actions, the act of visualizing actually causes our nervous system to act as if the action were taking place. By "practicing" in our nervous system we learn how to perform various actions. You experience this each time you think or visualize a scary or difficult situation. Watch your heart rate increase and palms sweat. Your nervous system believes the event is taking place. We now understand and can practice using visualization to improve our physical activities.

Learning to visualize your goals or various situations is not difficult. Visualization is an active use of your imagination. It is a skill you already possess, yet you can improve your ability with a little practice each day.

Let's say you are visualizing a scene from nature: either a place you've actually been or you can create one with your imagination. With your eyes closed try to "see" the scene as clearly and brightly as possible. Try to keep the image at eye level, or above, and as large as possible. Your attention will drift, but with practice you will increase your ability to use your imagination in a powerful, direct way.

Some people see the image as if they were looking at a large painting in a museum, or on a movie screen. Others like to actually feel themselves emersed in the scene. Take a few minutes and evoke a powerful and uplifting memory you have. What techniques are you using? Apply these same techniques each time you do a visualization exercise.

Try the following exercise. You can also improve your skill by visualizing places you've been or by evoking positive memories, "seeing" them, and trying to make them as clear and bright as possible.

Our self-image, how we "see" ourselves, can be improved through these type of exercises. Learn to visualize yourself in a positive way. Learn to feel comfortable with the image of yourself.

EXERCISE 9

Set aside ten minutes and use your ability to imagine and visualize, to go through, in your mind, a sport or activity you enjoy. You can watch yourself performing the activity or try to feel that you are directly experiencing the action. By visualizing the activity you are believing that you can do these actions and you are teaching your nervous system to do the actions perfectly. You will find that this even feels good! If you enjoy the freedom and excitement of skiing, you will find those same emotions emerging, even though you are only visualizing the activity.

Now let us move on to the more subtle realm of applying visualization techniques to the attainment of our life goals. Once we have learned to visualize simple objects or situations we can learn to visualize the goals we have set for ourselves. As an example, let us say that one of your life goals is to become a more confident person.

EXERCISE 10

Begin by visualizing something — a scene from nature, an animal or person — that for you exudes confidence. While visualizing, become aware of that "feeling" of confidence. Imagine you are breathing that feeling into yourself from the image you are visualizing. Allow the feeling of confidence you grow within yourself. Now visualize yourself sitting on a park bench on a sunny afternoon. Breath that confidence into the image of yourself each time you exhale. As you inhale, increase your awareness of the confidence within yourself. See the image of yourself as a confident person seated in the park on a sunny afternoon.

These types of exercises, and there are many variations you can create and use, open our minds to new possibilities and potentialities in our lives. Before we can become a confident person and enjoy all the ramifications of that in our lives, we have to be able to "see" or "believe" confidence within ourselves. That is exactly how the exercise helps us. This is the essence of visualization exercises. By our own volition we open ourselves to new and powerful realities in ourselves and in our lives. In this way we can use visualization to increase our ability to reach our life goals. At the end of this chapter I have noted the best book I have read on learning visualization techniques.

Why do these visualization techniques work? The act of visualization is an act of creation. There are many possible explanations, all equally valid, as to how this works. We do not need to know how the sun burns in order to enjoy sunshine. However, many people feel more confidence in something when they have a conception as to how things work.

We live in a universe of infinite possibilities. Each one of us has far more ability and potential than we believe. By visualizing we are opening our minds to a potential that has always been there, only we did not believe we could achieve it! Our potential is limitless; we only have to believe and act in order to achieve. Visualization is an aspect of belief. When we believe, we feel something exists or is real. By the dynamic act of visualization, we begin to bring into physical existence that which is still unmanifest.

The next question regards our possibilities. What are the farthest reaches of our potential? This question is at the heart of much spiritual inquiry. Some philosophies go so far as to say that we are God. Yes, you and I are actually the creators of all creation; we are also the creation.

Sri Chinmoy, in his description of "samadhi," a profound and deep level of awareness and consciousness, describes a realm where . . .

You see there that almost everything is done. Here in this world there are many desires still unfulfilled in yourself and in others. Millions of desires are not fulfilled, and millions of things remain to be done. But when you are in savikalpa samadhi, you see that practically everything is done; you have nothing to do.[1]

In "Nirvikalpa samadhi" an even higher realm, Sri Chinmoy describes an existence where . . .

There will be no ideas or thoughts at all. In nirvikalpa samadhi there is no mind; there is only infinite Peace and Bliss. Here nature's dance stops, and the knower and the known become one. Here you enjoy a supremely divine, all-pervading, self-amorous ecstasy. You become the object of enjoyment, you become the enjoyer and you become the enjoyment itself.

When you enter into nirvikalpa samadhi, the first thing you feel is that your heart is larger than the universe itself. Now you see the world around you, and the universe seems infinitely larger than you are. But this is because the world and the universe are now perceived by the limited mind. When you are in nirvikalpa samadhi, you see the universe as a tiny dot inside your vast heart.

In nirvikalpa samadhi there is infinite Bliss. Bliss is a vague word to most people. They hear that there is something called Bliss, and some people say that they have experienced it, but most individuals have no

*firsthand knowledge of it. When you enter
into nirvikalpa samadhi, however, you not
only feel Bliss, but actually grow into that
Bliss.*[2]

By glimpsing consciousness and our ultimate
potential from the vantage point described by
Sri Chinmoy as "samadhi" we open the door to
our untapped potentials. Once we understand
our unlimited ability, we realize that we need
only to conceive, believe, and act in order to
achieve.

Sri Chinmoy describes a realm where "everything is done." It would be comparable to
Socrates' realm of pure form where everything
exists in its innate perfection. Through the
power of our will, mind, emotion, and consciousness, we are able to enter this realm and
bring back a new "reality" into our lives. Once it
is manifested in thought, it will not be long until it appears physically. Our ability to visualize
is the bridge between the unmanifest and the
physical world. Visualizing and believing is more
than half the job.

It took a great visionary to set man's sights on
the building of the first skyscraper. Once the idea
was manifest, it was simply a task of planning
and building, which many people could do. The
great feat was believing and visualizing the first
structure.

Sri Aurobindo, one of the most influential Indian thinkers of the modern age, writes of humanity's potential for awareness and experiences in the following lines quoted from one of his poems:

I have become what before time I was;
A secret touch has quieted thought and sense.
All things by the agent Mind created pass
Into a void and mute magnificence.

Another poem concludes:

I pass beyond Time and Life on measureless
  wings,
Yet still am one with born and unborn
  things.[3]

We now begin to grasp the importance of visualizing and making as real as possible in our minds the things we wish to create. We are also beginning to feel and understand how this works.

A further description by Sri Chinmoy will help to solidify our awareness of this reality beyond our five senses.

There Infinity, Eternity and Immortality have become one. The Source becomes one with the creation, and the creation becomes one with

*the Source. Here the knower and the Known,
the lover and the Beloved, the slave and the
Master, the son and the Father, all become
one. Together the Creator and the creation
transcend their Dream and Reality. Their
Dream makes them feel what they are and
their Reality makes them feel what they can
do. Reality and Dream become one.*[4]

Here we find a merging of the concepts of
dream and reality. They become one. That which
we imagine or dream, and that which exists,
become one.

The challenge each one of us faces is to bridge
the gap between our potential and where we are
now. Mankind walks, lost in ignorance, not
knowing he is, in fact, both the creator and the
creation. The bridge between our reality and our
capacity is crossed by our conscious, dauntless
effort, or, as Sri Chinmoy refers to it, "our aspiration for perfection."

As we bridge the gap between our current
situation and our goal we will get, with each step
of progress, a sense of satisfaction. This satisfaction will inspire and encourage our continued movement towards our goals.

Many books have been written on the actual
techniques for visualization. *Using Your Brain
for a Change*, by Richard Bandler, is one of the
finest.

EXERCISE 11

Set aside ten minutes for this exercise. Imagine your goal clearly, visualize it in your mind. See it up close, with bright colors. Intensify the image. Feel it to be as real as possible. Hold that image and allow yourself to believe you have the potential to attain that goal. Self doubt will try to prevent you from holding the image. Allow yourself the freedom to believe, even if part of you thinks the goal or image is impossible. Dare to believe!

9

Action

Action is essential. If we do not act, we will not achieve. Through action we will begin the dawn of change. Change must take place if we are to reach our goals. It is change that we are seeking to create, or in a world of constant change, we may be seeking to create or maintain a constant. In either case, we are acting in order to have an effect in the world, to create our goals.

To act is to create an effect. Thinking powerfully, planning, feeling, and physical movement are all forms of action. Even though we may be sitting on a bench in the park we may be acting inwardly: doing away with negative thoughts, fostering a positive attitude, and focusing on our goals. Action is often incorrectly associated only with outward physical activity. This misconception is addressed by Sri Chinmoy in the following passage:

We have to see action in inaction, and inaction in action. What does this mean? It means that, while acting, we have to feel within ourselves a sea of peace and serenity. While we are without activity, we have to feel within us a dynamo of creative energy.[1]

After choosing a goal and a plan we begin to act, both inwardly, creating favorable attitudes and attributes, and outwardly, to affect change in the physical world. An essential aspect of learning to act is effectively learning to accept responsibility for our actions and the changes they bring to the world. The inability of individuals to take responsibility for their actions is one of the primary reasons our world is in such disarray. A sense of responsibility will add a power to each action that we perform. Responsibility comes with increased awareness and this awareness empowers and makes significant each action.

We may not have created the world or consciously created the situation into which we were born, but we are responsible. "Responsible" means the ability to respond. We have the freedom to respond, as we wish, to whatever situation we find ourselves in. By blaming others and cursing fate, we only weaken our minds and hearts. As we act and move towards our goals, we must assume responsibility for our actions and their results. This sense of responsibility makes us keenly aware of our power as individuals and the interconnectedness of all of creation. This responsibility applies to both thought and outer action. Thoughts are subtle actions. Sri Chinmoy:

> *We are our own fate-makers. To blame others for the unfavorable conditions of our lives is beneath our dignity. Unfortunately, this act of blaming others is one of man's oldest diseases. Adam blamed Eve for his temptation. Poor Eve, what could she do? She also blamed another. No, we must not do that. If action is ours, responsibility is also ours. To try to escape the consequences of our actions is simply absurd.[2]*

Again and again in this strategy for success we must return to the significance of the goals we have chosen. Our goal will dictate our plans and our actions. If our goal is not healthy, either to ourselves or to others, our actions will very quickly begin a string of unpleasant results. These results, or realities, are stemming from and created by our actions. We will, at some point, be called to respond to these creations of ours. We are responsible. We will have to respond to these unfortunate situations we have created, just as we will gladly respond to positive situations we create en route to positive goals.

We can run, but we cannot hide, from ourselves and our actions. To perform positive action towards goals that benefit ourselves and others will create a situation where we are blessed to respond and interact with positive situations. We will be called to respond and it will be a nice experience, much like planting a beautiful apple tree and then enjoying its beauty and fruits. The same will be asked of us regarding selfish actions and goals that harm the happiness of others. We will be called to respond. This is the essence of the idea referred to by Eastern philosophies as *Karma*. The essence of this idea is reflected in the Christian ethic: "as you sow, so shall you reap." An awareness of this idea of responsibility will give us the needed awareness of the great significance of the goals we choose and the actions we take towards those goals.

Once we feel confident in our goals and direction, we need to find a mode of action and an attitude towards action that will allow us to act as effectively as possible. Inaction is the worst of all.

To have only a goal and no action, either inwardly or outwardly, will be an unfortunate experience. We will quickly find ourselves living a life of wishful thinking and constant excuses. Inaction will create a void of non-growth. When nature does not grow, she becomes brittle and hard. Then she breaks and dies. We are part and parcel of nature. If we do not act and grow, our minds and hearts become brittle and hard. Unhappiness will soon result and unhappiness is an early form of death. We assuredly need to act.

Constant action requires a great deal of spontaneity and flexibility. Our plan, regardless of the care with which we have constructed it, is a fixed entity in a world always changing. This means that what works today may not work tomorrow. In order to keep acting towards our goal, we must be able to adjust our actions in accordance with ever-changing situations. In other words, admit when you've made mistakes, change your action, and keep going; admit when others' new ideas or information ought to create a change in your action. If your mind is rigid, your action will be rigid and hence unable to move swiftly and surely in an ever-changing world. Closed-mindedness and the inability to adapt to new ideas and situations will cause our actions to become closed and unadaptable.

Think of water, moving swiftly and surely around all obstacles, as it winds towards its goal. It is soft, changing, adaptable, yet swift and sure. Our mental attitude, which reflects our action and vice versa, must be the same. That which bends does not break.

In order to reach our goals we must be in action constantly. We have limited time to achieve that which we have placed before us. Our action needs to be swift, sure, and adaptable.

Without action decay sets in. Complacency, boredom, depression, anxiety, and lethargy will quickly befriend the inactive human being. A body of water without movement soon looses its ability to offer healthy, life-sustaining water. The same result occurs when our consciousness and awareness becomes stagnant. We lose the ability to nourish and sustain our spirit. We begin, essentially, to die. It is said that two deaths actually occur. The one no one sees, which is the death of our spirit, and the physical death.

By constant movement and action within ourselves and in the world, we flow like a mountain stream, fresh and alive, singing the song of satisfaction, as we rage ever closer to our goal, the limitless sea of human potential.

Effective action requires a well thought-out goal, a deep sense of responsibility for each action, and an adaptable frame of mind from which our action will emerge. Swami Vivekananda summed up these ideas quite well in the 19th century:

Those that blame others — and alas! the number of them is increasing every day — are generally miserable, with helpless brains. They have brought themselves to that pass through their own mistakes, and blame others; but this does not alter their position. It does not serve them in any way. This attempt to throw the blame upon others only weakens them the more. Therefore blame none for your faults; stand upon your own feet and take the whole responsibility upon yourselves. Say, "This misery that I am suffering is of my own doing, and that very thing proves that it will have to be undone by me alone." That which I have created I can demolish; that which is created by someone else I shall never be able to destroy. Therefore stand up, be bold, be strong![3]

10

Success and Progress

Success and progress will come to us as we move consciously through life. The joy of our journey will be intensified as we increase our awareness of issues seldom addressed when dealing with success. These are: understanding and cultivating a feeling for self-transcendence, choosing healthy goals, avoiding self-complacency, utilizing self-encouragement, and the need for constant peace and satisfaction in our lives.

The first step of our road to success was to choose a goal. If we work and act towards that end with determination, an adaptable plan, and positive inner and outer qualities, we will attain our goal. Success and satisfaction will be ours. At an unknown moment our goal will be realized.

As children our goal was to learn the alphabet. That attained, we turned our attention to whole words, then books, themes, ideas, and philosophy. One goal led naturally to the next. Sri Chinmoy writes of this ever-growing and expanding aspect of life.

> *Today we regard one thing as our goal, but when we reach the threshold of our goal, immediately we are inspired to go beyond that goal. That goal becomes a stepping-stone to a higher goal. This happens because God is constantly transcending Himself. God is limitless and infinite, but even His own Infinity He is transcending. Since God is always making progress, we also are making progress when we are in the divine consciousness. In the divine consciousness, everything is constantly expanding and growing into higher and more fulfilling Light.*[1]

As we learn to conceive and achieve, we become part and parcel of a never ending movement. Einstein envisioned an ever-expanding universe. As we become conscious and responsible participants in our own lives, we become aware of the web of consciousness of which we are an integral part. We expand as the universe does. Our goals and desires impel us towards that expansion. Today's goal becomes tomorrow's starting point.

By seeing this aspect of existence, we can begin to understand that our desires and goals are a natural impetus compelling us to enter into ever-greater dimensions of life and consciousness. We are expanding and growing.

A child feels hunger and eats. The child may not understand why hunger appears, but the simple desire for food and the feeling of hunger will ultimately help create a strong, healthy body, if the child takes action and eats. Our yearnings, goals, and desires are more than ends in themselves; when followed wisely, our goals will lead to far greater things than we can now imagine. The child will become an adult, a reality he may not even be able to imagine. The quality of growth will depend largely upon the type of foods eaten. The same applies to the desires and goals that we feed our consciousness. Healthy, balanced goals today will lead to a healthy, balanced life.

Complacency is a state of being that will detain us from becoming all that we can. As we reach each goal of ours, we must not become self-complacent, but instead immediately look out upon our previously unknown potentialities and seek our next goal. All too often people rest on their laurels and stop growing, learning, and expanding their levels of awareness and consciousness. Once we stop growing as individuals, we begin our descent along the road of closed mindedness and death.

If we are to successfully continue in our pursuits, we need encouragement. Oftentimes, due to a lack of oneness in the world, others may not encourage us, or even worse, they may become jealous of us. We must be sure to encourage ourselves. After each success we should acknowledge what we have done and be proud of our achievements, both inwardly and outwardly. Pride can take two forms: the pride that makes us feel superior to others will not help us in the long run. This is the pride of our small, egocentric awareness. The second type of pride grows within us from a feeling of self-satisfaction, achievement, and self-transcendence and will surely further our progress. This pride is our awareness that we are expanding and growing into our true potential. Only by transcending ourselves can we have abiding satisfaction. Sri Chinmoy writes:

The process of striving for perfection will never come to and end, because God Himself does not want to end His cosmic Game. Today what we feel is the ultimate perfection, tomorrow will be just the starting point of our journey. This is because our consciousness is evolving. When the consciousness evolves to a higher level, our sense of perfection simultaneously goes higher. Let us take perfection as an achievement. When we are a kindergarten student, our achievement of perfection may be very good for that stage. But from kindergarten we go to primary school, high school, college and university. When we get our Master's degree in perfection our achievement is much greater than what it was when we were in kindergarten. But even then we may feel that there are many things more that we have to learn. Then we will study further and enlarge our consciousness still more.

If the child thinks that the Master's degree will always remain unattainable, then he is mistaken. The spiritual ladder has quite a few rungs. If we do not step onto the first rung, then how can we climb up to the ultimate rung of the ladder?[2]

Competing with others dooms us to dissatisfaction for we are gauging our self worth on elements — namely the lives of others — that we cannot control. They have their lives, their purpose for living, and we have ours. Others can provide us with inspiration, but doing our personal best is all we can control and take responsibility for. The factors behind causation are often far beyond our control, so why use them as a means of comparison? Do not judge yourself by the achievements or opinions of others. Focus only on doing your absolute best. Think of someone who is a leader. Who are they to follow? They must look within themselves for direction. Another example is someone who is doing something that is no one else has ever done. There is no one else to compare oneself to. This person also can only do his or her best. If we adopt this attitude early on, it will create a mind-set and attitude that will increase manyfold our ability to succeed and progress in life.

Be aware also that satisfaction dawns not only when we attain our goals but also comes with every step we take towards our goals. Shakespeare said that to seek is more fulfilling than to find. If we do not experience the joy and happiness of every moment as we move towards our goals, then we will be missing the majority of our lives. The attainment of a goal is a momentary experience that soon grows old.

All too often people feel that happiness will dawn only when a certain goal is attained. This is a dire mistake. In essence, in soul and spirit, we are the same whether we possess a dime or a million dollars, whether we live a quiet, solitary life or live amidst the lights of fame and fortune. Our essence does not change. Life is ultimately an experience of becoming more conscious of our true nature. Our happiness and satisfaction in life will correspond to how close we can get to our essence. Happiness is what we all seek, though, in so many different ways.

We all want to be happy and happiness stems from peace. Peace within ourselves and peace in our lives. We have peace when we are satisfied with ourselves. We are satisfied when we are constantly expanding our minds, hearts, and lives. Our goals encourage us to do this, yet it is the actual moment of expansion that we must come to savor.

Spiritual teachers throughout the ages have stressed over and over again the importance of inner and outer peace. If we had truly listened to God's command, given to Moses thousands of years ago: "Thou shalt not kill," the world would be a far more peaceful, happy place. Sri Chinmoy writes:

No price is too great to pay for inner peace. Peace is the harmonious control of life. It is vibrant with life-energy. It is a power that easily transcends all our worldly knowledge. Yet it is not separate from our earthly existence. If we open the right avenues within, this peace can be felt here and now.

Peace is eternal. It is never too late to have peace. Time is always ripe for that. We can make our life truly fruitful if we are not cut off from our Source, which is the Peace of Eternity. The greatest misfortune that can come to a human being is to lose his inner peace. No outer force can rob him of it. It is his own thoughts, his own actions, that rob him of it.

Our greatest protection lies not in our material achievements and resources. All the treasure of the world is emptiness to our divine soul. Our greatest protection lies in our soul's communion with the all-nourishing and all-fulfilling Peace. Our soul lives in Peace and lives for Peace. If we live a life of peace, we are ever enriched and never impoverished. Unhorizoned is our inner peace; like the boundless sky, it encompasses all.[3]

If we depend on the actual attainment of goals to achieve our sense of peace, we may be chasing after a carrot that remains forever in front of us. We need to feel peace and happiness here and now with each step we take in life, as we wind our way towards our goals.

There are two aspects of each person: the eternal and the fleeting. Both must be embraced, here and now, to enjoy the full satisfaction of living. A Zen story tells of a monk describing the attainment of enlightenment, "Before enlightenment chop wood, carry water; after enlightenment, chop wood, carry water." The joy and fulfillment are waiting for us in each moment, in every experience we have.

Therefore let us enjoy each step we take along the journey towards our goals. This attitude will hasten the attainment of our goals. Happiness and satisfaction are magnets that attract further happiness and satisfaction. A great journey begins with the first step. In that moment of the first step, the entire journey is embodied. Allow yourself the joy and satisfaction of each step confidently and powerfully taken.

The End

Notes

Chapter 1

1. Matthew 6: 32–34.
2. Sri Chinmoy, *Eternity's Breath*, (New York: Agni Press, 1975), p. 38.
3. Swami Nikhilananda, *Vivekananda: A Biography*, (New York: Vedanta Press, 1989).
4. V.S. Naravane, *Modern Indian Thought*, 2nd Ed. (India: Asia Publishing House, 1967), p. 178.
5. *Eternity's Breath*, p. 19.

Chapter 2

1. *Modern Indian Thought*, p. 177.
2. Ibid. p. 249.
3. Ibid. p. 250.

Chapter 3

1. Ibid. p. 135.
2. Sri Chinmoy, *Beyond Within*, (New York: Agni Press, 1985), p. 98.
3. Ibid. p. 79.
4. Ibid. p. 144.
5. Abraham H. Maslow, *Religions, Values and Peak-Experiences*, (Penguin Books, 1983).

Chapter 4

1. Sri Chinmoy, *Yoga and the Spiritual Life*, (New York: Agni Press, 1974), pp. 96–97.
2. *Modern Indian Thought*, p. 141.
3. *Beyond Within*, p. 47.
4. *Vivekananada: A Biography.*

Chapter 5

1. Sri Chinmoy, *The Illumination of Life Clouds, Part III*, (New York: Agni Press, 1974), pp. 18–19.
2. *Vivekananda: A Biography*, p. 190.
3. *Beyond Within*, pp. 142–143.
4. *Vivekananada: A Biography*, p. 191.

Chapter 6

1. *Beyond Within*, pp. 157–158.
2. Sri Chinmoy, *Meditation: Man-Perfection in God-Satisfaction*, (New York: Agni Press, 1987), p. 107.
3. *Vivekananada: A Biography*, p. 190.

Chapter 7

1. *Beyond Within*, pp. 165.
2. Ibid. p. 213.
3. Ibid. p. 217.
4. Ibid. p. 191.
5. *Vivekananda: A Biography*, p. 190.
6. Ibid. pp. 190–191.
7. *Modern Indian Thought*, p. 180.

Chapter 8

1. *Meditation: Man-Perfection*, pp. 283.
2. Ibid. pp. 284–285.
3. Sri Aurobindo, *Last Poems*, (India: Sri Aurobindo Ashram Press, 1952).
4. Sri Chinmoy, *Kundalini: The Mother Power*, (New York: Agni Press, 1974), p. 24.

Chapter 9

1. *Yoga and the Spiritual Life*, p. 10.
2. Ibid. p. 27.
3. *Vivekananda: A Biography*, p. 191.

Chapter 10

1. *Beyond Within*, pp. 13–14.
2. Ibid. p. 516.
3. *Yoga and the Spiritual Life*, p. 13.